DOORS2

Photographed and compiled by
BILL & MARNIE BREHM

Copyright © 2014 William A Brehm

All rights reserved.

ISBN: 0973866942
ISBN-13: 978-0973866940

Cover: Trinity College, Dublin, Ireland

DEDICATION

To Theodore Geisel
who said
"The more that you read,
The more things you will know.
The more that you learn,
The more places you'll go."

Bunratty Castle, near Shannon, Ireland

Obsessed by a fairy tale, we spend our lives searching for a magic door and a lost kingdom of peace.

Eugene O'Neill, American playwright

Ireland

My grandmother had this high-tech security system – a rusty nail she used to lock the door.

Quincy Jones, Jazz trumpeter and composer

Ireland

When the strong box contains no more, both friends and flatterers shun the door.

Plutarch, Greek historian

Limerick, Ireland

When I was a lad I served a term
As an office boy to an attorney's firm.
I cleaned the windows and I swept the floor,
And I polished up the handle of the big front door.
I polished up the handle so carefullee
That now I am the Ruler of the Queen's Navee!

Sir William S. Gilbert, HMS Pinafore, English Librettist

Stirling Castle, Stirling, Scotland

"Why it's simply impassible!
Alice: Why, don't you mean impossible?
Door: No, I do mean impassible. Nothing's impossible!"

Lewis Carroll, English author, *Alice's Adventures in Wonderland & Through the Looking-Glass*

Mom, Neenah, Wisconsin

"The door', replied Maimie, 'will always, always be open, and mother will always be waiting at it for me."

J.M.Barrie, Scottish Author, *Peter Pan in Kensington Gardens*

Edinburgh, Scotland

The most sacred thing is to be able to shut your own door.

> G. K. Chesterton, English author and philosopher

Waterford, Ireland

The longer one hesitates before the door, the more estranged one becomes.

> Franz Kafka, Czech-Austrian author

Malahide, Ireland

I find that when you open the door toward openness and transparency, a lot of people will follow you through.

US Senator Kirsten Gillibrand

Kirkwall, Orkney Islands, Scotland

Knowledge of what is does not open the door directly to what should be.

>Albert Einstein, German-American theoretical physicist

Edinburgh, Scotland

There is always one moment in childhood when the door opens and lets the future in.

> Graham Greene, English author, Nobel Prize winner

St. Kitts, West Indies

Once my heart was captured, reason was shown the door, deliberately and with a sort of frantic joy. I accepted everything, I believed everything, without struggle, without suffering, without regret, without false shame. How can one blush for what one adores?

George Sand, French author

Dingle, Ireland

I love shutting my front door and being at home with just my dog and me. That's when I'm happiest.

Lucy Davis, English Actress

Edinburgh, Scotland

I have this complex that if I walk into a place wearing a colorful shirt someone will stop me and say, 'I'm sorry, but the Latin band comes through the other door.'

Oscar de la Renta, Dominican-American fashion designer

Royal Mile, Edinburgh, Scotland

An actor entering through the door, you've got nothing. But if he enters through the window, you've got a situation.

Billy Wilder, Austrian-American filmmaker

Edinburgh, Scotland

But first, the news: The House of Commons was sealed off today after police chased an escaped lunatic through the front door during the Prime Minister's question time. A spokesman at Scotland Yard said it was like looking for a needle in a haystack.

Ronnie Barker, English comedian

Princes Street Gardens, Edinburgh, Scotland

Journalism can go right up to the door of the room in which the decisions are made. A novel can go inside the room – and inside the characters' heads.

David Frum, Canadian-American political commentator

Medieval house in historic park, Ireland

I don't want a door bell. I don't want anyone ringing my door bell…seems to be intrusive. They can call me on their cell phones.

Malcolm Gladwell, Canadian author

Medieval Museum, Waterford, Ireland

Follow your bliss and the universe will open doors where there were only walls.

> Joseph Campbell, American mythologist-author

Kirkwall, Orkney Islands, Scotland

And as she looked about, she did behold,
How over that same door was writ,
Be bold, be bold, and everywhere Be bold.
At last she spied at that room's upper end
Another iron door, on which was writ
Be not too bold.

Edmund Spenser, English poet, *The Faerie Queen*

Kirkwall, Orkney Islands, Scotland

Not many sounds in life, and I include all urban and rural sounds, exceed in interest a knock at the door.

Charles Lamb, English writer and essayist

Bunratty Historical Park, Ireland

Footfalls echo in the memory
Down the passage which we did not take
Towards the door we never opened
Into the rose-garden.
My words echo
Thus, in your mind.

> T. S. Eliot, American-English playwrite-essayist

Rosslyn Chapel, Roslin, Scotland

Then cherish pity, lest you drive an angel from your door.

> William Blake, English poet and painter

Glasgow, Scotland

Put me on a train mama
This place just ain't the same no more
Put me on a train mama
I'm leavin' today.

3 Doors Down, American rock band

Royal Mile, Edinburgh, Scotland

He was thinking alone, and seriously racking his brain to find a direction for this single force four times multiplied, with which he did not doubt, as with the lever for which Archimedes sought, they should succeed in moving the world, when someone tapped gently at his door.

Alexandre Dumas, French author

Kirkwall, Orkney Islands, Scotland

Many miles away there's a shadow on the door of a cottage on the shore of a dark Scottish lake.

Sir Walter Scott, Scottish historical novelist

Bunratty Historic Village, Ireland

Never bolt the door with a boiled carrot.

Irish Proverb

Irish Cottage

Close the door, you don't live in a barn!

> Midwestern USA Mother's Saying

Killarney Castle, Ireland

Drive out prejudices through the door, and they will return through the window.

> Frederick II, King of Prussia, in a letter to Voltaire

Tobermory, Scotland

It's doors I'm afraid of because I can't see through them, it's the door opening by itself in the wind I'm afraid of.

Margaret Atwood, Canadian author, *Surfacing*

Calton Hill Park, Edinburgh, Scotland

Charity begins at home, and justice begins next door.

> Charles Dickens, English author

Dublin Castle, Dublin, Ireland

Luxury is the wolf at the door and its fangs are the vanities and conceits germinated by success.

Tennessee Williams, American playwright

Dingle, Ireland

I can walk into the front door of any factory and out the back and tell you if it's making money or not. I can just tell by the way it's being run and by the spirit of the workers.

                        Harvey S. Firestone, American businessman

Listowel, Ireland

The haven from sophistications and contentions
Leaks through its thatch;
He offers succulent cooking;
The door has a creaking latch.

> Ezra Pound, Expatriate American poet

Dublin Castle, Ireland

The love of our neighbour is the only door out of the dungeon of self, where we mope and mow, striking sparks, and rubbing phosphorescence out of the walls, and blowing out own breath in our own nostrils, instead of issuing to the fair sunlight of God, the sweet winds of the universe.

George MacDonald, Scottish author, poet and Christian minister

Dublin, Ireland

Every person is a new door to a different world.

John Guare, American playwright, from *Six Degrees of Separation*

Dublin Castle, Ireland

Vice came in always at the door of necessity, not at the door of inclination.

Daniel Defoe, English writer, from *Moll Flanders*

Dublin, Ireland

Every now and then one paints a picture that seems to have opened a door and serves as a stepping stone to other things.

> Pablo Picasso, Spanish artist and Cubist

Dublin, Ireland

He who listens at doors hears more than he desires.

French Proverb

30 William Street, Waterford, Ireland

The greatest step is out of doors.

German Proverb

Waterford, Ireland

If you deal in camels, make the doors high.

> Afghan Proverb

Waterford, Ireland

Treat people as if they were who they ought to be and you will help them to become what they are capable of being.

Johann Wolfgang von Goethe, German writer and statesman

Waterford, Ireland

Creativity is contagious, pass it on.

Albert Einstein, German-American theoretical physicist

Munster Bar, Bailey's New Street, Waterford, Ireland

Charlie Munster is a scoundrel and a con-artist from way back. Why, the doctor who put him together didn't have an honest bone in his whole laboratory.

                Herman Munster, Character from "The Munsters"

Waterford, Ireland

Midnight, one more night without sleepin',
Watchin' till the mornin' comes creepin',
Green door, what's that secret you're keepin?

Marvin Moore, American Lyricist

Isle of Man, British Crown Dependancy

It's official, highway patrolmen are not susceptible to the Jedi Mind Trick.

> Stephen Colbert, American political satirist and comedian

Isle of Man, British Crown Dependency

The will to win, the desire to succeed, the urge to reach your full potential… these are the keys that will unlock the door to personal excellence.

Confucius, Chinese philosopher

Tobermory, Scotland

The wind sae cauld blew south and north, and blew into the floor; Quoth our goodman to our goodwife, "Gae out and bar the door."

Medieval Scots ballad

Skaill House, Sandwick, Orkney Islands, Scotland

The doorstep to a great house is slippery.

Irish Proverb

Skaill House, Sandwick, Orkney, Scotland

To be nobody but yourself in a world that's doing its best to make you somebody else, is to fight the hardest battle you are ever going to fight. And never stop fighting.

e.e. cummings, American poet

Kirkwall, Orkney, Scotland

He comes inquiringly to our door, seeking the new birth, and asking withdrawal of the veil which conceals divine truth from his uninitiated sight.

Albert G. Mackey, Mason, The Manual of the Lodge

Stirling Castle, Stirling, Scotland

For so it is written on the doorway to paradise that those who falter and those who fall must pay the price.

Victor Hugo, French author *Les Misérables*

Stirling, Scotland

It's a dangerous business, Frodo, going out your door. You step onto the road, and if you don't watch your feet, there's no knowing where you might be swept off to.

J. R. R. Tolkien, English author, *Lord of the Rings*

Stirling, Scotland

What is opportunity, and when does it knock? It never knocks. You can wait a whole lifetime, listening, hoping, and you will hear no knocking. None at all. You are opportunity, and you must knock on the door leading to your destiny.

Maxwell Maltz, MD, American author of *Psycho-Cybernetics*

Edinburgh, Scotland

As I walked out the door toward the gate that would lead to my freedom, I knew if I didn't leave my bitterness and hatred behind, I'd still be in prison.

Nelson Mandela, South African, Anti-apartheid revolutionary and Nobel Prize Winner

Rosslyn Chapel, Roslin, Scotland

It takes as much energy to wish as it does to plan.

> Eleanor Roosevelt, American First Lady and political activist

Edinburgh, Scotland

Poetry is the opening and closing of a door, leaving those who look through to guess about what is seen during the moment.

Carl Sandburg, American poet

www.ingramcontent.com/pod-product-compliance
Lightning Source LLC
Chambersburg PA
CBHW041802160426

43191CB00001B/5